The Fool and the Physician

ANDY BROWN is Director of Creative Writing at the University of Exeter. His most recent books of poems are *Goose Music* [with John Burnside], *Fall of the Rebel Angels: Poems 1996–2006* (both Salt Publishing) and *The Storm Berm* (tall-lighthouse, 2008). A short selection of his work appears in the anthology, *Identity Parade* (ed. Roddy Lumsden, Bloodaxe Books, 2010). He was previously a Centre Director for the Arvon Foundation at Totleigh Barton and is a poetry tutor for the Arvon Foundation and the Poetry School.

Also by Andy Brown

POETRY

Goose Music (Salt, 2008, with John Burnside)
Fall of the Rebel Angels: Poems 1996–2006 (Salt, 2006)
Hunting the Kinnayas (Stride, 2004)
From a Cliff (Arc, 2002)
The Wanderer's Prayer (Arc, 1999)
West of Yesterday (Stride, 1998)

CHAPBOOKS

The Storm Berm (tall-lighthouse, 2008)
The Trust Territory (Heaventree, 2005)
of Science (Worple, 2001, with David Morley)
Vital Movement: Reality Street 4-packs No.4
(Reality Street, 1999, contributor)
The Sleep Switch (Odyssey, 1996)

AS EDITOR

The Allotment: new lyric poets (Stride, 2006)
*Binary Myths 1 & 2: correspondences with poets
and poet-editors* (Stride, 2004)

The Fool and the Physician

by

ANDY BROWN

SALT
LONDON

PUBLISHED BY SALT PUBLISHING
Acre House, 11–15 William Road, London NW1 3ER, United Kingdom

© Andy Brown, 2011

The right of Andy Brown to be identified as the
author of this work has been asserted by him in accordance
with Section 77 of the Copyright, Designs and Patents Act 1988.

Salt Publishing 2011

Printed in Great Britain by the MPG Books Group, Bodmin and King's Lynn

Typeset in Swift 9.5 / 13

ISBN 978 1 84471 346 2 paperback

This book is for Corinna Wagner

1 3 5 7 9 8 6 4 2

Contents

Acknowledgements

Thanks are due to the editors of the following publications where these poems, or versions of them, were first published.

Agenda for 'The Departure'
Ekleksographia for 'Clown in Space', 'The Clown's Prayer', 'Egg Register', 'Clown in Heaven', and '*Zugunruhe*'
Orbis for 'A Circus Paradelle'
Shearsman for 'Jeroen van Aken' and 'Chimeras'
Stride Magazine for 'The Fool on the End of the World', 'The Cure of Folly' and 'Hieronymus Bosch'
This Line is Not For Turning: The Anthology of Contemporary British Prose Poetry for 'Clown Alley'

Three books in particular have been very useful in researching Bosch's paintings: *Bosch*, Robert L. Delevoy (Skira/Rizzoli. New York: 1990); *Hieronymus Bosch*, Carl Linfert (Library of Great Painters. New York); and *Hieronymus Bosch*, Ludwig von Baldass (Thames and Hudson. London: 1960). Several phrases in this collection may well be inadvertently indebted to their scholarship.

Acknowledgements are also due to the University of Exeter for the time and support to research and write these poems.

'At forty, every man is a fool or his own physician.'

TIBERIUS

'If the fool would persist in his folly he would become wise.'

WILLIAM BLAKE

I. A Clown in the Moonlight

Clown in Space

In September 2009, Canadian clown Guy Laliberté, founder of the
Cirque du Soleil, *was launched into space from the Kazakhstan*
steppes.

Above the steppes I career into space
and wonder myself into darkness.
It is daytime down there, 'broad daylight'
up here, but utterly dark. Below on earth
the atmosphere spins the sunlight into gold,
whilst up here there's no atmosphere at all
to strike a glow between the stars—
there is nothing like darkness to remind you
you are extraordinarily alive, and alone.

The blue planet turns like a plate on a stick
underneath the Heavens' billowing Top,
slung with a billion fairy lights and spots.
The stars perform their hypnotism act,
pulsing like the cities down below.

Although I'm the first of my kind into space,
my friends are all around in constellation:
Leo jumping through his ring of fire;
the Gemini twins in bareback balance,
riding round the ring on Pegasus;
the giant Betelgeuse and his team of red dwarfs;
the Sisters of the Pleiades, holding on
like the Severinis in their human pyramid.
Here is Orion, throwing knives at Venus,
and Hercules decked with his barbells and furs.

Impossible to juggle here—the balls simply float
from your hands, although tumbling is easy:
you set yourself in motion, spinning round
and round and round.
                                    But this show is soon done
when Earth obscures the blue-eyed moon;
when my dreams slide down the thrilling slopes
of the Big Dipper; when the lit-up world floats by
and this audience of one returns to gravity
and stumbling jokes, as the ring-master Sun
calls closing time on the *cirque du soleil*.

The Clown's Prayer

> In the prison of his days
> Teach the free man how to praise.
>
> W.H. AUDEN

Oh Lord, oh Harpo Marx, oh Charlie Chaplin: glory be to the insanity itself, for it is divinely inspired, it is carnival. Glory be to the messengers of mayhem, the anarchists, the silent performers. Glory be to the red flannel coxcomb and bells. Glory be to doing things the wrong way round. Glory be to juggling with a small dog at our heels. Glory be the mystery that deceived the Devil; the glee that leaps across our lives.

Oh Joseph Grimaldi, oh William Kempe, oh Pantomimus: where there is a rope on the floor let us wrestle it like a snake. Where there is a donkey or a pig, let us ride it home backwards. Where there is pomposity let us criticise the master and his guests; let us make fun of, be indelicate about, and rude towards, without fear of reprisal. Let us kill ourselves with laughter. When we stumble over the edge, commit us to imperfection.

Oh Harold Lloyd, oh Lou Costello, oh Oliver Hardy: blessed is he who trips across the line between the man he is and the man he would be. Blessed are they who float in the workaday world. Blessed are they who show what is wrong with the way that things are. Blessed is he who takes the pie in the face and gets knocked on the arse. Blessed are they who spank the crowd with a slap stick.

Oh Coco the Clown, oh Stan Laurel, oh Bud Abbott: teach me to wear freckles, warts, a big red nose. Teach me to stand in for the lion tamer; to touch freely on the touchiest issues. Teach me to look at myself in the mirror and find the trickster in a domino mask. Teach me to glance through the windows of the world I've missed. Help me be mischievous, not malicious. Teach me to 'Sweep Up the Spotlight'.

Oh Puck, oh Nick Bottom, oh John Cleese: make me nimble and able whilst clumsy and dim. Help me mingle ecstasy and death. Make me the keystone that holds up normality's arch. Help me to be wise enough to lead the deadpan troupe. Make me a tramp in patched and tattered clothes, then make the others do my bidding. Help me set up scenes that turn out droll. Make me wise enough *to play the fool himself.*

A Clown in the Moonlight

'There is nothing funny about a clown in the moonlight.'
LON CHANEY

How we feel about the clown
depends on where we see him—
a circus or party, no problem,
but ringing your doorbell at sundown?

That clown is a psycho killer,
a mirror of your fears,
knocking the world out of kilter . . .
and his laughter? It shears.

Zugunruhe
'*migratory restlessness*'

As the quickening caravans bore us north
across the city's borders, we forgot
those staring eyes behind the wires,
the wildness of the weary bears and lions.

As we crossed the city's borders we forgot
that departure itself was a sort of hope.
The wildness of the weary bears and lions
and cheering crowds evaporated.

Departure itself *was* a sort of hope:
some knelt and kissed the dusty road
where the cheering crowds evaporated.
Such exits are a part of our story.

Some knelt and kissed the dusty road,
praying for safe arrival and tomorrow's show.
Such exits are a part of our story:
they make sense of us, as a path the forest.

Praying for safe arrival and tomorrow's show
those staring eyes behind the wires
make sense of us, as a path the forest,
like the caravans bearing us quickly north.

A Circus Paradelle

We drove off in the caravans that evening.
We drove off in the caravans that evening
to find the places not marked on our maps.
To find the places not marked on our maps
that marked evening, we drove our caravans
off (not on) the maps, to find the 'In Places'.

But for each other we might never have found
that line in the distance. Was it morning?
That line in the distance; was it morning?
But for each other we might never have found
the distance in the line. But for that morning
we might never have found it was each other

on the surface of well-trodden roads.
On the surface of well-trodden roads
our other selves, cawing in the pines.
('Our other selves, cawing in the pines').
In the well-trodden pines, our selves,
cawing on the surface of other roads.

We drove off in the caravans that evening
on the surface of well-trodden roads,
to find the places not marked on our maps.
But for each other we might never have found
our other selves, cawing in the pines.
That line in the distance; was it morning?

Clown Rondeau

In circus rings the clowns' coarse show
delights the bleachers row by row—
the crowd goes wild, while in the sky
the acrobats like angels fly
serene above the heads below.

'We are the fools; just days ago
we lived like you, saw sunsets glow,
laughed and were loved, but now we die
to make *you* laugh in circus rings.

'Take up our quarrel with the foe!
To you from battered pails we throw
torn papers; be yours to hold them high!
If you break faith with us who die
for laughter's sake, we'll no more go
into circus rings.'

Sad Clown Triolet

Inside the ring the clowns run faster,
though all the audience now has gone.
Their show was a complete disaster
inside the ring.
                    The clowns run.
                                    'Faster!'
cries the spiteful circus master—
he'll see them punished until dawn
inside the ring. The clowns run faster.
And all the audience now are gone.

Ballad of the Fool

As I walked home from Old Gastown
I met a man who was a clown—
his attitude was pure Piltdown,
 to ridicule.

He grew up in a shantytown
where water stood a stagnant brown
and all the shacks were tumbledown
 as a rule.

But his politics were thistledown
as he worked his way to a suite uptown
and became a boss who was renowned
 as cruel:

when the workforce put their gizmos down
and struck for pay or work slowed down
he laid off half, knocked wages down—
 divide and rule.

But he bought his wife an eiderdown
of silk and gold, a diamond crown,
and a Christian Dior ballgown
 on a whim last Yule.

I saw him last at the works' hoe-down,
his two left feet were letting him down
as he danced to soul and old Motown.
    It wasn't cool.

He died that night in a park, midtown,
when laid off workers brought him down
with a hammer weighing twenty pounds
    then threw him in the pool.

I knew a man of ill renown
whose attitude was upside down
and brought about his own shakedown.
    The bloody fool.

Portrait of a Man Falling Over

He plunged, the way a book falls down,
     alighting on its spine,
his pages fanned for all the world to see.

Clown Alley

'Why is the clown so sad?' the small girl asked herself, as she
tiptoed through the ruined curio shops outside the circus
compound. It had been raining all day and, although it
was late and she was contented, her hat and clothes were
mud. A crow flew down and landed on the fence behind
her shoulder.

'Maybe he isn't sad at all,' the bird replied. 'Maybe he's happy
and it only sounds like sadness, because you hear it
through sad ears.'

'You mean to say the clown is really *happy*?'

'I don't know. Why don't you ask him yourself?' The
scavenger of reason flew away.

The girl, with gracious eyes, approached the clown. 'Clown?'
she said. The clown looked up. 'You lonely?'

The clown considered what she'd asked and smiled. 'Everyone
must chop through Time,' he said, 'playing, working,
making others laugh. Yet what is that but a one way loop
that leads to becoming a forgotten man? After the rush
to the centre of the ring, the *ricorso* to the solitude of the
road . . .'

The small girl shuffled her shoes. 'What must one do to be a
clown?' she asked.

'Why, one must *be* a clown, of course!'

'And what *is* that?'

'To remain in incredible light, yet embrace its promised
darkness; to forget the present in favour of tomorrow;
to never forget that the world is there and that everyone
is people, even you. One must be alone—no soul for
days—and open one's eyes to the yawning heart of
things . . .'

That's more like it! the small girl thought.

[15]

'And one more thing,' the clown went on.

'What's that?' The little girl, intrigued.

'A secret.'

'Being . . . ?'

'When you're out there throwing knives, always aim with purpose for the heart.'

Haiku

The clown sits in the kiosk
sharpening his wit
on tourist dollars.

Clown in Heaven

You enter Paradise only once: a circus of gaudy facades, vast caravans filled with working troupes, old weather-boarded hoardings up on high, canvas cupolas, pot-stoves and fairy lights. Once you've stepped out of the tunnel, you're going to be supremely happy here . . .

The First Heaven is bounded by a fence of coloured bunting. You enter at the end of time across the worn-down steps, where the eyes of the pale concierge — that master of deflation — light up. Half-smiling, half-crying, he signs you in, hands out the hats, and shows you to your seat up in the bleachers. Only those who died laughing are granted entrance or, *sola fide*, those who have always believed in the Ringmaster.

The Second Heaven is a tent of pure silver, and there the stars, each with its warder, are hung out like spotlights on golden chains, shining on you as the audience applauds. You enter here the realm of the fallen angel, Punch — *Pulcinello*, that young chicken, making mincemeat out of children, battering policemen, devils, crocodiles, and bullying long-suffering Judy. They make for splendid hosts.

The Third Heaven is an arena of gold and black. You enter when it is full dark, the censers swinging like lanterns at a feast. This is the domain of Harlequin and Columbine. Harlequin is invisible to all, and dances through the clouds frustrating those who fall for his beautiful wife, *for whom you will fall*, in memory of your human warmth, the cold wind of your passing and of your final unmasking.

The Fourth Heaven is a three-ringed tent of pearl, echoing to the laughter of angels, white as jasmine. You enter on the Monarchs and their Jesters: Sir Dagonet, Patison, Patch; John Scogan and old Will Somers; Robert Grene and his Virgin Queen. Here sits Muckle John, the Angel of Death, writing in a ledger, or scribbling out—the former the names of those persons new-born; the latter the names of the newly deceased.

The Fifth Heaven is of white gold, and is Bottom's. Here dwells the Angel of Asses, whose height is 500 days' journey, and who brays ceaselessly for the sins of man. You enter to a riot of burlesque masques, obscene dances, jests, indecent songs.

The Sixth Heaven is a Green Wood and is Puck's. Here resides that Avenging Angel who presides over all of his minions: Trinculo, Grumio, Launce and Speed; Dromio, Costard, Touchstone, Lavache; Dogberry, Pompey, Yorick and Feste. You enter that place where the manna is made that feeds the life eternal.

The Seventh Heaven is formed of light beyond the power of tongues to describe. You enter on the Throne of Glory, under which lie all unborn souls. Each soul is bigger than the whole circus and has 70,000 heads; each head 70,000 mouths; each mouth 70,000 tongues; each tongue blowing 70,000 raspberries, forever employed in hallowing the praises of the Most High.

Clown School

When teacher tells you, 'Find your inner clown'
don't blush; to find the marks of your own two feet
amongst the muddled foot prints on the road
is not so hard . . . she's asking you to be
the sphere that knows the centre of its mass;
to find those parts of you that lie like seeds
in cracks; to be the trembling drop of dew
at the grass blade's tip; to think of yourself
as something you could skate on. She wants you
to explode with laughter amongst your friends
or know, perhaps, what a creature might do.
She's asking you to store these gifts like fire.
Remember, she just wants you to become
a stack of jumbled driftwood on the flow.

Fool Street

Down on Memory Street men and women prune
the trees at the ends of their wild gardens,
each one a connoisseur of autumn leaves,
whilst over there on Adolescent Street
boys tremble on the verge of their girls' lips.
On Nostalgia Street the widespread malaise
is tied to the future with chains. Over
on Restaurant Street they put it on your bill,
whether you ate it or not, bread or milk,
whilst up on Honey Street they fly between
flower and hive and serve it free to all
who watch them play those hard fought games of chess
they undertake on Competition Street.
The many minds of Pluralism Street
are working on the problems thrown up by
the international strife on Terror Street
where the blatant war on fear goes on and on
and the folks of Gone-Without-a-Trace Street
look for ones they loved who simply vanished.
On Love Street life has much that is still French
about it, but its rumours and murmurs
could hail from any land. Perhaps a girl
will pass you here and enthral you with her
carefree shrugs and nods as she ascends
the time-worn steps that lead to Dreamers Street.
On Marriage Street they walk with both hands tied,
whilst on Forgiveness Street they throw themselves
prostrate upon the ground. Way over there
on Future Street a step extends as far
as a mile, crossing the horizon to
no-one knows precisely where. Ah the things

I could tell about Promise Street, but won't . . .
On Clock Street all is fixed whilst far away
the bells of transformation are chiming,
but down on Stasis Street there is no change.
All things seem possible when one is in
Prospect Street: always, everywhere, you are
under some kind of spell. It's difficult
to get a visa back into the past,
but on History Street you can. Even in
the so-called new quarter. On Garden Street
the buildings' roofs are lush. To see the blooms
here is to remember all the poems
you have ever read and to remember
the poems is to tread the perfumed map
that leads you to the songs of Meaning Street.
On Song Street each outpouring of music
takes you to an old haunt you frequented.
Silent Street is more sedate, like Dead Street
where the deceased—those unbreakable threads
whose spirit is embodied in the living—
emerge each day and stick around till night
rooted in the minds of those who work here.
Where else but in Body Street do they bask
so fully in the physical? Mind Street,
with its tenor of coolness and reason,
can't lay a claim to titles such as that.
What's this across the road on Mirror Street?
That would be us, of course. On Present Street
each moment is a gift; don't waste your batch.
On Zen Street apprentices rake gravel
by a smoke-filled temple and moon-filled pond.

Inside their heads they move the kind of rocks
that keep one-and-all on Reality Street
embedded in the dusty world of things.
It's easy to get lost in Translation
Street, with its signs in foreign languages.
Language, bipedalism and tool craft
are all the rage on Evolution Street
and in the taxidermic cases of
Museum Street you'll locate the dead zoo
of stuffed beasts that all the children adore.
Maybe I shouldn't have, but Sceptic Street
proved alluring and there I lost my way.
I worked the answer out on Question Street:
soon I'd be heading back home to Fools Street
where life sinks through the spaces in between
the struggles each day delivers. It is
a fine morning. I think I'll walk the streets.

Egg Register

A clown joins *Clowns International* and turns up at the offices to register. Her features are blanked out with white-stick: a love-sick and melancholy *Pierrot*. Here she can patent her make-up design, her character, clothes and set routines.

'Many kids dream of becoming a clown,' the secretary says, 'but being a clown takes more than you'd imagine. At circuses, the local fair, or children's birthday parties, the clown must willingly fall through that hole between slapstick and salvation. Anyone can make a person laugh, but a true clown has to raise the charm each time she puts her costume on. It's not just comic wigs and outsized shoes; it's not just tumbling and pratfalls, a fight with a collapsing chair. It isn't only squirting flowers, rubber chickens, custard pies, confetti buckets, tripping over your own two feet, or too many jokers climbing out of a minuscule car. No. It is a state of being; being someone who can make you smile no matter what the cost. It means running your life, daily, down the knife edge of humour and chaos. You know there are some tribes for whom the ceremony cannot begin until the clowns have made each person laugh . . .'

An eggshell is decorated as a miniature version of the clown's head: her ears are painted red. The other features, in green and black, are brushed on delicately. The egg is added to the *Egg Gallery*, as a kind of clown copyright.

All Clowns Exit Running

The name of a set clowning routine

What happened to it all; to the gorgeous marquee;
what happened, years later, to all our rapport?
When the canvas was ripping did you hold up the poles;
what happened when the big top began to fall?

What happened when it was puddles *every day*;
when thunderheads broadcast those non-stop storms;
when the rain ran so deep and our jokes turned to rust
and the waters cut off our way back home?

We wandered the wastes under festival signs.
We snagged our clothes and raked our skins.
'How did *that* happen?' the sad troupe asks,
'How did we not notice oh so many things?'

Pretending to be Me

mask (noun) from the Arabic *maskharah*—*clown*.

I

I don my mask and feel like me once more;
I'm two faced, a Janus, inverting truth
and illusion, closing the door on the past

and opening the future; a hybrid
of me and not me—my indecent nose,
the lips laid on thick, this ludicrous grin.

I'm a pantomime mummer in blacked-out
disguise, the mock king of the masquerade,
unleashing confusion at centre stage,

reaching beyond politesse and yardstick.
I clutch my *marotte*, my precious mannequin
and see in his features my own second self.

Behind this static countenance of grease-paint
that covers up as much as it reveals
lives *the other me*, lurking like somebody

who broke into my house. I enter the party
across the threshold, walking on my hands,
my ragged hobo's clothes on inside out . . .

II

But isn't this what we spend each moment doing:
'pretending to be me', letting our speeches form
a fragile skin that covers us from birth to old age,

death? And if there is a choice to be had, only later
will we find the answer, when the skull is bare
and it's too late to do much about it, if at all.

Over the years and decades you get to know
these patterns are randomly written. Some days
it's all amusement, the balm of good medicine,

or stories of a fêted amphitheatre where
we pick up the threads of our life with the fortune
of an alchemist turning lead—like that!—to gold.

Until then we keep heading on, looking back
until something new arises, our arms
spread wide towards our own emerging image,

or we set sail with wine, good friends and a song,
guided by our luck and lunacy, the glimmer
of moonlight like the mask of memories

that delivers us from being someone else.
But for now there's still that speck of light,
a blip on the radar up ahead, guiding us

home to ourselves, to the visible world
that comes of itself each day, warmed up
by the faith we attach to love's lingering fires.

The Lord of Misrule

The Lord of Misrule
at the Feast of Fools
turns the world upside down
as the Christmas clown . . .
        O I am the Lord of Misrule.

The Lord of Misrule
at the Feast of Fools
is the master of revels
at a table of devils . . .
        O I am the Lord of Misrule.

The Lord of Misrule
at the Feast of Fools
is our chosen marauder
of the social order . . .
        O I am the Lord of Misrule.

The Lord of Misrule
at the Feast of Fools
owns the whole paraphernalia
of this wild saturnalia . . .
        O I am the Lord of Misrule.

The Lord of Misrule
at the Feast of Fools
makes life topsy-turvy
and his masters unnervy . . .
        O I am the Lord of Misrule.

The Lord of Misrule
at the Feast of Fools
runs the drunken melee,
makes the whole world obey him . . .
　　　　O I am the Lord of Misrule!

But the Lord of Misrule
at the Feast of Fools
masks something much darker
behind the anarchy . . .

The Lord of Misrule
at the Feast of Fools
suffers death by the knife
as the year's sacrifice . . .

The Lord of Misrule
at the Feast of Fools
dies by fire, or by blows,
or the oak tree's gallows . . .

Yes the Lord of Misrule
at the Feast of Fools
makes masters serve slaves,
but digs his own grave . . .
　　　　O who'll be the Lord of Misrule?

The Fool on 'The End of the World'

It's the end of the worm as we know it,
it's the end as the hungry thrush feeds.
It's the end of its wounds and its worries.
    It's the end of the worry beads.

It's the end of the wort as we know it
just as we start slaking our thirst.
It's the end of the words of the wordsmith.
    It's the end of the Würst.

It's the end of the workouts we practised,
it's the end of the worldly as well.
As the worthy make way for the worthless,
    it's the end of what's worthwhile.

It's the end of the worm as we know it,
it's the end as the hungry thrush feeds.
It's the end of its wounds and its worries.
    It's the end of the worry beads.

II. The Fool and the Physician

A series of poems based on a selection of the works, and life, of the Flemish master painter Hieronymus Bosch.

The Garden of Earthly Delights

The poem is composed using only words spelled with letters from the title of this painting.

I

It is early, first light. The land glisters.
The grey of night has lifted, all signs
of hoarfrost gone. The earth is gently
heating, idling into its daily goings-on,
its grasses and daisies starting a fresh
heritage and history at the steady rate
they alone feel. Day floods itself and gains
a holdfast on the air's near stillness
ordaining the onset of rising deeds.
Here in the shire, in this foreign field
near Flanders, the Netherlands—this England
or Ireland; in this Italian glade; in Andorra
and Estonia, Finland and Georgia, or north
in Greenland, or yet in the Indian East—
day slides into dale and glen. The *terroir*
stirs to the rise and shine. Light finds inroads
on the region, highlighting the ridge
at the lane's end. No railings, gratings,
gates or grilles here; the land is totally
free. Sited on the fringe of these fells
there is no shortage of gelid floes
to refresh and rinse the soil and stone.
This is no arid desert for only the driest
thorns and gorse. Nestled in this grange,
nets of tendrils thread the grassy sod;
sedges, leafy hostas, tiny trefoils,
godetias and teasels green the fords

[35]

and dingles. Foliated fronds, forsythia,
asters and alders, firs and ferns, aloes,
sloes and horsetails—all raise a floral riot
at the lido's edge.
                        And then stirring
to feed on their leafage, an antlered hart
and his roan doe; a stag and his hind.
A grey heron alighting on her nest, dines
on frogs and froglets, straggling toads;
angelfish and shoaling goldfish; hydra.
Dragonflies dart here and there. The ants
are diligent in their forts. Hares dash.
A glossy otter says *adios* to her holt.
Lions and tigers snarl and roar. Snails
slither along on their shiny trails.
Forty feral dogs and dingoes lose their
leashes and the herds of horned horses
lose their halters too, as they neigh, snort
and flare their nostrils in the early rays.
A grey titan, large-eared, his nose a hose,
lends a gorilla a ride to the shore,
as a line of tiny foals and geldings strides
near the rooting hogs and hedgehogs,
the regal griffins, the rhinos and rheas,
the shaggy goats shooing off their fleas,
the train of listless tortoises,
all noted in the eyes of the aloof giraffe . . .

II

and in the air a great gyrating S
  of the feathered sort:
    golden orioles, graylag geese,
      garganey, starlings and teal,
      goldeneye, ganders,
        goosander and eider,
      little egrets, great egrets
      rail, dotterel, sanderling, stint,
     royal, roseate and sooty terns,
    rollers, redtails,
fieldfare and harriers,
  long-tailed tits,
    great tits,
      throstles
    and a golden
   eagle,
its talons
flashing.

III

As in a giant silo grain on grain
is stored, so here heads and torsos
throng together instantly, load on load,
a sodality of all sorts, of all trades
and all lands; a solidarity of nations:
Netherlanders, English, Irish, Italians,
Algerians, Assyrians, the Senegalese—
these and others gather at a gentle gait
at first, then hotfoot it along the shingle,
shooting along the shores and sand,
flying along the inlets and islands,
the leats and islets of these green leas,
to hang onto one another on the strand.
A yard of granite fonts and hydrants—
slate grey, rosy, indigo—slosh onto
the gritty shelf of silt in this inshore sea,
frothy litres falling in a foggy rain
on the rallying host. As a tide drains
off the shale and flint or the groynes
at the seafront, so they filter to this tarn
and float in dinghies, sit adrift on rafts,
or ride in a ring astride horses and hogs.
Yet no saris or sarongs adorn those
gathered here at these ghats, no dhotis.
No one is shod in shoes, or gaiters,
nor galoshes. No one has on threads
of satin nor of yarn. Not a shred
of linen here. No shifts or stays,
nor a dirndl dress in sight. Here are
no grandiose togas or togs, little finery.

No singlets or shirttails, shirts or ties;
no leotards or hosiery, thongs or girdles.
There are no hats to see—no fedoras
adorn these heads—only a host of
angels dressed in haloes. No one snags
their fishnets, for there are no fishnets.
The sartorial fashion is different,
the style one and one alone: Flesh

       Radiant Flesh!

IV

Tall and short, little and large, fat and thin;
lithe and lean tanned legs, shins,
a density of thighs,
fine feet, toes and nails,
heads and hairdos,
shorn, longhaired,
redheads in ringlets;
teeth and grins,
flashing eyelids,
dilated eyes,
elfin ears,
long lashes.

Yes, there is no dearth of it—here are fans
of the flesh galore! They dot the fens
and aisles in drifts, setting-to on one another.
The grandest lords and ladies need no intro,
the grottiest tailors and hordes of fools
get it on *sans* nattering, *sans* a hint of ego.
No one here is selfish in their ardor.
They are not trying it in theory, rather
getting it on firsthand. And as for toil?
There's no one hoeing the soil here;
no grinding the nose to the stone, no heat
at the forge. They all forget yesterday's
tillage in the fields, the gathering-in
of silage, and earn their festal rights
in the doing. Dishrag and doily are tossed
aside; all is gaiety—flags flying at the fiesta.
Heralds heft their ensigns to sail in the air . . .

V

Listen . . .

          their ringing *ding dongs* signal
the start of the daylong orgy. Friends
and strangers of all ages yearn together:
sirens and sires, yogis and yoginis,
ying and yang—one half of the other—
hedonists, realists and royalty. Earls
say fond *Hellos* to their yielding serfs;
shoot eyes sidelong for a honeyed sight.
Lodgers yell *Hey There!* to loafers;
senators stroll alongside sentries
and soldiers freed of drafts and sorties.
Gaolers greet gentry. Handsels and Gretels
dash free of the forest. Heroes and heroines
get in a fling. Doyens of the stage
and dairy girls entertain hale goatherds;
dainty gals enthral daft gents and headstrong sons.
A senhor holds a nosegay to his hot senhorita—
she inhales the fragrant tang of his fan
of tansies, roses, selfseal, heartsease
and lilies, a tinsel of foliage. Other noses
sniff at resins and oils redolent of neroli . . .

VI

This is a synod of the saintly and sinners,
the honest, the false and the fallen—
for there is no real sin here, only delight:
a seraglio of harlots and helots, feisty
geishas, old hags snogging teen lads,
hoydens, sheilas, nosy hidalgos.
These horny legions! They are solid gone;
in altered states! Are they all in sedation,
high on ergot, stoned? In the throes of
their glee, not one of these is silent;
there are no stifled *oohs* and *aahs* here,
only an hysteria of sighs and groans,
the strains of a strange-fired yodelling.
Altos sing glorias—*legato*, *largo,* then
heartily. A tenor sings songs to his dear;
there another reads his idol his Idylls,
his *andante* rondels and odes, his riddles.
Ariels sit astride their ditsy lads singing
the notes of a ditty. Dishy sailors sing,
not dirges, nor litanies to a tragedy,
rather a shanty, to the faint tones of a lyre,
or the stranger tones of a sitar—*shanti shanti.*
Adonis, alongside his darling, toes a tango.
A sonneteer offers his other half sonnets
and, to adorn herself, a string of garnets,
girasols. As a heist of golden florins
shines, so these shine. As English groats
and farthings glint, so these glint. As gold
ingots and inlaid gilt earrings glisten,
so these glisten . . .

There is no thrift
in this fresh air salon, nothing's on ration,
the tents are food-laden—fare of all sorts
lies arranged for the eating: figs, oysters,
hen's eggs in saffron, honey, fresh dates,
roasted onions, shallots, garnish. They drain
the dregs of their flagons of ale, taste tea,
eat *gelato*, a giant *fraise,* hide in giant eggs,
in larger-than-life shellfish. One goes
foraging for *girandoles.* One hoards stores
of sage and sorrel, a sheaf of oats and rye
to share. One brings trays of oranges,
raisins, radishes. They dine on a fragrant
loaf of star anise, feasting on all the nosh.

VII

And soon they are in a right lather,
engaged in relations of all sorts.
They are all after one another;
after a roll in the hay. No one is alone
or left aside, none are estranged.
Here are no onanists sitting on their tod.
No one is ignored, lonely, isolated.
All are integral. No one dithers.
They are all in on it; free agents.
None are staid. Their sole desires?
To gird their yearning loins
and enlist for these gifts of gladness.
Yet this is not altogether English
this ethos of Eros and all it entails! . . .
there is a randy fire in their glands;
their arses are rosy, their groins oily.
The day is instantly glistening genitals,
fannies and glans, a slit here, tits there,
glorified yonis and dongs aligned and
realigned; long fingers find holes, hands
toss off engorged organs, frig hairy dens.
One is angling to get laid; she toys
on the haft of her lad's rod and teeters
on the edge of a fine disorder. All
sangfroid gone, he has the hots for her.
As she readies herself she softens
and sits on the length of his thing.
It rends her senseless. She loses
her sense of reality. He rises rosily,
stands astern her. His horn inflates,

as hard as iron, digs in. He gyres
and rides her, shifting gear, faster.
He shafts her in fresh artistry.
She rolls off and readily steels herself,
is antsy for another fan. A gifted florist
inserts foliage in another's rear end.
He has the horn, is the horniest.
He hits the tangy target. One ogles.
One is lost in the heat of fellatio.
One fastens easily to a girl's tail,
hones his rod and grinds. One slithers
into the safety of a shell, half-hidden
in its shady interior; another shelters
in a glass hose; yet others are enthroned
in great glass lenses, as if at an altar
or dais, a shrine to their deity; as if
they held the holy grail, the *sang real*.
They all feel defiantly filthy, these rites.
Hardly has one finished his teasing
than a girl finds herself ardently fondled,
as if on a rota. They flirt in the dirt;
are lost in heady energies, strong feelings.
Rather as a tin of sardines is filled
to the edge, so they lie in tight layers,
in tangles, in trios, stirred in desire, a-fire.
Eighteen or eighty, they do it in great élan
these slathering generations. Shagging is rife.
Oral. Gay and hetero. One girl longs for
another—she is in range—she gooses her,
fondly darts her fingers in, finds a finger-hold;
the deft rotations she has learnt. She dies

[45]

the little death. She feels her rear, lies on her,
flogs her—the sting of her leathering.
Fiddling and toying reign. Tingle, tingly.
One saddles her lad—steadily he hardens,
fits his entire girth inside to the hilt. She
eases herself onto it as if seated in yoga.
His entry into her triangle gratifies. Gently
she slides it into her folds. He stares
into her steady eyes. He's a good lay,
a stellar ride; she's glad to nail her date.
It sends her into elation. He enters her holes;
she enters his. They shift roles, holder to held,
holding tight, tied together, hogtied, snared.
They are hinged together at the front.
She delays shooting her load as her heart rate
rises. One slogs, one adroitly slithers,
one shyly adores, one is agile, one alert,
one fidgets, one flits, one is in the agonies
of his grand finale, one faints, one flashes
in nifty flair, one soars in death defying
feats of titillation, one nods in doting elation,
one dangles for a dare, one raises the ante
and hoists his gal into the air—he handles her,
holds her aloft, startles her, steals her,
she has a soft landing at his side
in the heart of this great to-do.
Yet do they start to lag in energy?
Are they all a little sore? No.
All these hornily energised feats
only edify these adherents of Eros.
They inherit a heresy so tantalising,

all reason has fled and only the legit
delights of the flesh are left, a trillion-fold.
They rend a gash in the order of things,
a rift in the salient ordinariness of life—
they are godlier as they engage.
This heartening idea grants healed hearts;
leans ladders against the air and lifts
anyone here to glory to loftier heights,
to *Satori*, to a different sort of *Tao*.
It lifts the lid on sanity and seals their fate:
a hotline to god, to the higher grade,
this ideology of satisfied thirsts.

VIII

And they *are* satisfied
                              that no dire fiends,
nor Hades' desolate foes are here on raids,
gross in the foetid gas of dingy fens,
to infest this neat garden, this tidy yard,
to detain and destroy in their gory gnashing.
They *are* satisfied that no ghastly horrors
are fallen here to erode the ideals of these
intense lads and lasses. No rash of oafish ogres
stands treating the fiords as a latrine;
no strange ghosts loiter at the font;
no irate satyrs giggle as they set fire to tinder,
singeing the terrain to a nasty nadir.
All fright, all grief and hate, all rage and ire
are fended off. Only the genial gather here;
in this theatre of the flesh's glories.
They fight off strife, lethargy and sloth.
Nothing negates or tarnishes their relish;
nothing strangles their ardor, nor trashes
their gladness. Here, in this foyer to glory,
all the ghastly ordeals of ordinary days,
all the grisly trials and feints of stale reality,
are translated into sheer delight.

IX

At the end of it all they settle on one another
as ash settles after a fire, softly and in heat,
and later still they'll all tell tales and stories
of the day's astonishing goings on, as they
head for the hayloft or a night in a hotel.
And in all these dealings does anyone get
a dose? After the orgy, are they tinged
in sadness and deflation? Does angst arise?
Does anyone fret that these forays are fragile,
a fad? Does anyone lose faith in the flesh?
No. None are denied their needs. None feign
their heights. Today, as the last light dies
and the heat starts to fade there is no danger
anyone is tired: yesterday they did it together
and then today . . . and tonight . . . and again . . .
these rites that see off the dead shall go on
for aeons, this era of desire, day after day.
No sooner does it roll to a halt than it restarts:
their destiny, their fate, their grand design,
yearlong, year on year. Yes, Yes, Yes, oh Yes.

The Adoration of the Magi
after W.H. Auden 'Musee des Beaux Arts'

What we do results from where we are—
emerging from the landscapes of our lives
and of our dreams—just as what happens
in this world happens, mostly, without us,
unnoticed in the distant emptiness, where
the future hangs like something long forgotten.
We do not know what goes on and what we do
we often times ignore.

                              As in Bosch's painting
The Adoration of the Magi, for instance:
how everything turns away from the unmoved
town at the mouth of the river, fringed by those
familiar dunes, where a traveller is mauled
by wild animals and a woman chased by wolves
through the blasted trees and untamed land,
their suffering ignored or passing unnoticed
in the wider details of the indifferent earth;

or how everything turns from the rotundas
and stupas of our homely town, turns away
from the ruinous gallows and the horsemen
galloping beneath the ensign of the moon,
insisting, instead, that *this* is all that matters:

how here there came on the fourteenth day
three Kings and Magi following a star, here
to this decrepit inn under the sign of the swan,
where Joseph kindles a modest courtyard fire
and a shepherd couple sprawl indecently
rubbing their eyes in the smokescreen
of ceremony;

how *this* is all that is the case,
rather than the truth of robbers hiding out
in wait for us somewhere in the spreading land,
or how each day oscillates between delight
and joy and other signs of unrest, violence:
the surface that could split at any time.

The Ergotist

As Athanasius tells it in his *Life*,
or the hagiographic masterpiece
the *Legenda Aurea*, so here the man
himself in *Ignis Sacer*—Holy Fire.

> *The blight comes on the rye stem*
> *(a cock's spur on the grass stalks)*
> *in the moist days after harvest*
> *in the cool and spreading lowlands.*

'And tell me of your symptoms?
The convulsions, itching, headaches.
Do you vomit? Is there gangrene
in the fingers? Dropsy, loss of limbs?'

> *The blight comes on the rye stem.*

'And tell me of your visions?
Have you mania, psychosis,
and hallucinations? Do you feel
a sexual longing, or bewitched?'

> *(A cock's spur on the grass stalks.)*

I'm a hermit in the desert:
pestilence and tragedy,
black magic, beasts and weird fiends
swarm through the anxious countryside

> *in the moist days after harvest.*

The devil's envoy brings a letter
side saddle on a giant mouse,
an invitation to the blazing village,
delivered to a strange disorder

    in the cool and spreading lowlands.

The alchemist is at his still,
the devil in his stove-pipe hat;
a witches' Sabbath watched by owls
in darkness underneath the scuppered bridge.

    The blight comes on the rye stem,

a riot of phantasms masked as men
who seek to overwhelm my faith.
Unholy revels, malefic spells;
a brothel in a giant's ass . . .

    (a cock's spur on the grass stalks).

They carry me into the air
prostrate upon a wingéd toad,
flying fish and monkey ships
sail through the sky like magic carpets

    in the moist days after harvest.

The only thing that's certain here—
a fabric of uncertainties.
A pig-faced priest who mumbles psalms,
dead tree trunks enclosing the living

in the cool and spreading lowlands.

They tempted me with money, lust,
a naked woman bathing in a stream—
erotic queen of hocus pocus.
Yet I prevailed with self-denial, prayer:

The blight comes on the rye stem
(a cock's spur on the grass stalks)
in the moist days after harvest
in the cool and spreading lowlands.

Jeroen van Aken

'It's 1516. My sixty-third year
in Hertogenbosch, this cloth and iron town
remote from the heart in Northern Brabant.

My wife and I live out our final days
in a world full of infidelity,
laid low by sin. For ten years I've painted

nothing, though I've seen our churches burning,
flaming river banks, villages on fire,
towers toppling here and there through thin ice,

Hell erupting from underground, each rock
pierced by trees—trees lifting up rocks—dark eyes
and ears listening from under a stone.

I am as a stranger in my own time:
like a dried-up riverbed that runs through
a deeply fissured land, its recessed crags

steep above the mild plains, then out beyond,
along the desolate coast where tall ships
smoulder and go down in the curving bay;

or closer still where birds of day chase off
the predators of night who roost inside
the hollows of a giant human tree.

The crescent moon of unbelief hangs high,
a glint in the night, like the eyes of owls,
of magpies or of swans, or moist-eyed toads . . .

and though the peaceful Lowlands lie around,
corruption spreads as far as men can see.
The world cares nothing for one man's torments—

this morning in the street where charlatans
make livings fooling lords and fine ladies
with conjuring and hocus-pocus, where

beggars and cripples scrape the dust for coins,
I watched a dupe refill his leaky jug
at the village pump: he cranked the handle,

water flowed, his pots drank every drop,
and yet the level never rose for all
the cracks that crazed the bottom of his flask.

We are actors in our own dumb routines;
gullible peasants in makeshift shelters,
vagabonds sleeping at doorways to caves,

wanderers in temporary dwellings.
A man crawls into a beehive in vain
hoping to find rest. Frail children set out

to sail their scuppered boats upon the stream
and drown. What threatens us, we made ourselves.
The end is imminent—terrors close in —

so why do they refuse to mend their ways?
The fortunes and misfortunes of a man
reach past memory and presentiment.

As when the inconceivable bursts through
the surface of our lives—when the inside
becomes outside—so all is upside down.

The burghers are fools, concerning themselves
in sensual pleasures and frivolity,
black witchcraft, devilry and alchemy.

They dance a zigzag path through the public
spectacle, forgetting it was a clown
who last died on the gallows, on the wheel.

How did the pantomime of skeletons
in cages come to be so trivial?
The uniform of folly's worn by all.

It is 1516. Righteousness fights
with temptation; punishment with reward.
Turn away from the things of the world. Turn

back to Time's passage to eternity.
Hold fast in hand your pilgrim's cockleshell.
Hold fast still, Brethren of the Free Spirit.'

The Forest that Hears and the Field that Sees

The field has eyes,
The wood has ears.
I will see,
Keep silent and listen.

FLEMISH PROVERB

But yet the peaceful forest scene remains
deceptive . . . all this blossoming, of course,

as we stretch out on the grass, or on a slab
of moss, trailing our fingers in the stream

in light of the meadow between the trees,
those alder, birch and rowan that give way

onto the gentle slopes of hills and cliffs—
a tranquil spot to meditate, perhaps—

but the twisted roots and hardened stem are
always close at hand; the thorn bush

at whose base the linnet's body lies, cold,
inert, its stomach full of baneful seed.

> Where the fox lies in wait for the cock hen
> not all things seem so undisturbed or calm.

The Departure

i.m. Dereke Leslie Brown, who taught me to be wise, saw me being foolish,
and let me work out for myself which was which.

I

Shrunken, gaunt, you lay like a saint
penitent in his ruined sanctuary,
strewn with relics, crumbling slabs.
The broken past lay deep inside
the hollow of your heaving chest
asking to be repaired with each
defiant rasp. Holding on, I told you
all about the birch tree in *my* yard,
reminded of the birch tree in your own
we sat beneath in summers long before
caution made you cut the giant down.
The present recedes into the past
the way a landscape shifts: the browns
and greens so close up; distant blues.

II

You were heading to your distant city,
with that *plenitude of bliss*; the peace
that comes of self-command, or maybe
just acceptance, as at the end of an illness,
no longer lost in delirious dreams, staring
fixedly at nothing—what mystics call
the contemplative state. You were gone.
But for those of us who had to stay
'getting away from earth a while' was no
option—the real and evanescent world
keeps coming back to touch, and back

[59]

to mind. It erupts through skins, the thin
veneers with which we keep it covered:
like the face rising from the pool before us.

The Haywain

'The world is a haystack; and each man plucks from it what he can'
— PROVERB

'All flesh is grass'
— ISAIAH

Riding the hay wagon home: the copious yield
at summer's end, the good harvest brought in . . .
or is it? Who shares in this abundance?
Pitchforks and ladders, we scramble on board,
fighting over fistfuls, unaware of what
we want, nor what we will do when we get it.

The VIPs process—Minister, Banker, Boss—
their spokesmen riding over the have-nots:
a throat slashed here, a chest stabbed there,
the vain troupe in pursuit of its illusions.
This cart will not decay in some chocolate-box
corner of a farm, but drives on to its unsure
destination. And when it has gone, what remains?
The mountains and the distant sea. Fields of flesh.

Ship of Fools

Despite the talk of storms we went out sailing
and three drinks down were all soon in our cups.
When something cracked, you asked if we were ailing

and whether something serious was up.
Were we now underway, or run aground . . .
but we were three drinks down and in our cups.

We picked up mermaids on our ultrasound.
Was that more storms ahead, or was it sunny;
were we now underway, or run aground?

When lightning hit our mast it wasn't funny,
the mermaids disappeared beneath the waves.
Was that more storms ahead, or was it sunny,

would we all end up in a watery grave,
or would our simple vessel stay afloat?
The mermaids disappeared beneath the waves

singing 'Fools set out to sea in unsound boats'.
Despite the talk of storms we went out sailing.
Would our simple vessel stay afloat?
When something cracked, you asked if we were ailing.

Rhyme

Hieronymus Bosch, Hieronymus Bosch
    your scenes of Hell are quite a squasch,
    packed with both the poor and posch . . .
Hieronymus, Hieronymus, Hieronymus Bosch.

Hieronymus Bosch, Hieronymus Bosch
    you caught them in a colour wasch
    to point-up folly and all the tosch . . .
Hieronymus, Hieronymus, Hieronymus Bosch.

Hieronymus Bosch, Hieronymus Bosch
    the human race is all awasch
    and screaming O good golly gosch . . .
Hieronymus, Hieronymus, Hieronymus Bosch.

Ecce Homo

I

Scourged before the loutish mob—
ravenous for blood and settling scores—
he stands inspected by the frenzied force
in this theatre's frozen moment.

Ecce Homo! a cautious Pilate cries
from the stage of the chambers of judgement,
its bitter cold flagstones inflamed by the horde
beneath him in the pit. His words hover

above the wild-tongued bonnet of the Pharisee
who thrusts his captive forward; above
the wild-tongued hydra of the crowd
whose hatred spreads like rumours—

    those harmless rumours in the harmless streets
    of the far-off city with its kindly bazaar,
    its amiable clusters in the public square
    beneath the flags and inviting blue roofs—

yet here across the rundown bridge,
across the filthy stream where drunkards puke
and clueless children race their battered boats,
men sneer and jeer in approbation: *Crucifige eum.*

II

'By your actions you have forfeited
your right to live freely in society.
You are hereby sentenced to death . . .

by Boiling, by the Brazen Bull,
to be Broken on the Wheel, or Buried
Alive. To be Burned.

To wear Cement Shoes and Colombian Necktie.
To be Crucified, or Crushed. To die
by Decapitation by Axe, Sword, or Guillotine.

To be Devoured by Tigers and Lions; by Dogs.
To be Disembowelled and Dismembered.
To be Drowned. Electrocuted. To die by Elephant

or by the Firing Squad. To suffer
the Five Pains: removal of the nose, hand, foot,
castration, then severed at the waist.

To be Flayed, or Gassed. To die by Hanging Cage.
To be Hung by the neck 'til you are dead—
the Long Drop or Short Drop. To be Drawn

and Quartered. To commit Harakiri.
To be Immured, Impaled. To meet the Iron Maiden.
To die by Lethal Injection, or by Lynching.

To die by Necklacing, Pendulum, or Poisoning.
To be Quartered by Horses.
To be Sawn in Half, or die by Scaphism.

To be Slow Sliced—the Death of 1,000 Cuts—
and suffer a Slow Strangulation.
To be thrown in the Snake Pit.

To die by Spanish Tickler, or by Spanish Donkey.
By Starvation. By Stoning. By Throat Slitting.
To be Thrown From the Tarpeian Rock.

Do you have anything to say
before sentence is committed?'
          Salva nos Christus redemptor.

Fools for Christ

It's enough to make you want to give up all
your worldly goods and whirl round like a Sufi;
to flout convention like a Holy Fool

and hit the road to Damascus with Saint Paul,
or talk with beasts, like Francis of Assisi.
It's enough to make you want to give up all:

to walk like Isaiah, barefoot, naked, tall;
to live like Dave the Dendrite up a tree
and flout convention like a Holy Fool.

Ezekiel lay before a stone and called
on God, who bade him bake his bread on faeces.
It's enough to make you want to give up all

you know, to talk in tongues, or even crawl
to Mount Kailash. Go 'crazy for God'. Act goofy.
To flout convention like a Holy Fool

just snub your worldly cares and act screwball—
dumb-down on purpose; join the *Yurodivy*.
It's enough to make you want to give up all
and flout convention, like a Holy Fool.

The Seven Deadly Englynion

Cave, Cave, Deus videt — Beware, Beware, God sees thee.

I

Is it so bad to be a man of leisure?
Do feasts and snoozes cause offence to Measure?
When conducted thoughtfully, both
Gluttony and *Sloth* can bring great pleasure.

II

These I've committed: *Sloth*, *Gluttony*. Oh, and *Pride*.
I've also tried *Lust* and *Anger*. But *Envy*—
that dumb show of jealousy—
like *Avarice*, is not for me.

III

I have to say I'm quite a fan of *Lust*:
rolling in the dust or revelling like Pan
on moor tops, in the sea, or on the sand
with a picnic, wine, my girl, a fruity flan.

IV

This eye of god, its pupil fringed with rays
of light, gazes on you as you binge—
or so they would have you believe. So cringe
or accept it: you're caught in your own *springe*.

V

A friend of mine complains that 'Men in suits
are camp'. I disagree. The point is moot.
These days I'm vain enough to want no more
than to hit the floor in new tweeds and new boots.

VI

So this is the way that the world goes to pot;
in hot-headedness and lack of composure?
But *Anger*'s seen me through some tricky mo's
and brought a sticky row or two to close.

VII

This painting's made as an *Imago mundi* —
where the mundane and the devil's cargo
fuse in a delicious farrago
of licentiousness *à gogo*.

Chimeras

A cyborg is a cybernetic organism, a hybrid of machine and organism
. . . The cyborg is a creature in a post-gender world.

DONNA HARRAWAY, *A Cyborg Manifesto*

Apple-shaped women (triangle downward)
have broader shoulders compared to their hips;
compared to their levers, their pulleys and tackle.
Apple-shaped women have rounded machines
with multiple cannons, completed in copper,
mounted on wheels of turtle design,
powered by enormous treadmills, steam,
or horses. Apple-shaped women have slim
legs and thighs. Their bellies and chests
can seem out of proportion. Fat is mainly
spread across the tummy, face and bust.

The *ectomorph* is small framed and thin
with narrow shoulders, hips and slots
to view the enemy. He may have trouble
gaining weight; he may have a *ballista*
with several springs, a level bar, a cog.
The ectomorph has trouble building
muscle, a braking system, or solid shields
of wooden planks. An ectomorph needs
to eat as much carbohydrate as he can
to become a one-man battleship, or rocket-
powered cannon-ball that flies ten thousand feet.

Banana (or rectangular) women have waists
nine inches smaller than the hips or bust.

Banana-shaped women are rotated by screws,
sail-powered tanks, by spikes and pitons.
The wheel-lock systems and scaling ladders
of banana-shaped women have scythes
joined to their chariots at the rear. The body fat
of banana-shaped women is spread around
the abdomen, buttocks, chest and face.
This creates the typical ruler. Their shells,
filled with gunpowder, explode upon impact.

  The *mesomorph* is normal weight: neither
  fat nor skinny. He packs on muscle easily,
  stands angled to absorb the force of recoil
  with his system of gears attached to driving
  wheels. He can lose weight easily, is more
  than just a shell, with room enough for a man
  to sit inside and aim his mid-range barrel.
  He has shoulders wider than his hips;
  breech-loading cannons arranged around
  the rim of his wheels. As they rotate
  he arches and discharges each radial bow.

Pear or bell-shaped women (triangle up)
have hips much wider than their busts.
Fat distribution varies, with fat tending
to deposit in the buttocks, hips, and thighs.
Women of this type tend to have a (relatively)
large rear, robust thighs, a small(er) bosom,
flexible arms bent back with ropes or a winder
mechanism to power the penetrating effects

of missiles hurled against the city walls.
Body fat is spread around the waist, the upper
abdomen and underneath the armoured plates.

   The *endomorph* is considered to be
   pear shaped. Meaning his hips are wider
   than his shoulders; meaning by striking a pin,
   by turning a winch, or pulling on a rope
   he can gain weight easily and is curvy;
   meaning that he is cast in iron or bronze
   and that his cranks attached to trundle wheels
   allow him to sling a grappling hook across
   the walls. An endomorph should eat less
   carbohydrates. An endomorph has four scythes
   attached to his machine, like helicopter blades.

Hourglass women (triangles opposing,
facing in) have hips and busts of (almost)
equal size, with narrow waists, bridges
and battering rams. Their body fat is spread
around both upper and lower abdomen.
This body type enlarges arms, chest, hips,
before the waist, which sits built into
a brazier of coals. When their water turns
to steam, it drives a rack of fourteen guns
arranged in tiers, striking them with hammers
from two remote-control firing mechanisms.

Hieronymus Bosch

Oh subsonic rhyme:
your 'Shh' combines
his roomy bunches.

Hey sonic rhombus:
my chino rosebush
is chosen by humor.

Oh bunchy isomers:
my shrub cohesion
obeys micron hush.

Hush nosy microbe:
his shrub economy
is bushy on chrome . . .

his choosy number
hums bony heroics
in mushy brooches . . .

> his bunchy Romeos
> buy him schooners
> on my birch houses!

Our Boyish *Mensch*!
Such bony heroism!
Such homey robins!

I bunch my horses.
I rush honeycombs.
Cue boorish hymns.

Curse on a Wedding

Take Bride & Groom, straight-backed beside each other
with downturned gazes. Place a sorcerer

at the altar to conduct proceedings
with vials and flasks. Hire a bagpipe-playing

witch, to pour her potions down the gullets
of any revellers who might collapse.

An inky swan who belches acrid plumes;
an arid, spit-roast hog spitting venom;

two dirty dogs to bash your diners' legs
while, outside, all those uninvited guests

bash at the gates. Now last of all, within:
a conjuror making water out of wine.

In time the spell you've cast will run its course
from marriage; house; to two-point-two. Divorce.

The Cure of Folly — a definitional poem

Meester snijt die keye ras.
Myne name is Lubbert Das.

Master, hurry, remove the stone!
My name is [the fool] Lubbert Das.

O man who owns or has control of a dog,
horse, or other domesticated animal,
please remove from my head
the hard, solid, non-metallic substance
that rocks are made of
(as is used in building materials),
with great speed
because of a real or perceived want of time,
for I am somebody considered to lack
good sense or judgment
and I go by the appellation Lubbert Das.

O person highly skilled at something,
let me encourage you to act
with even greater speed
and excise from the topmost part of my body
where the brain, eyes, nose, ears, mouth
and jaws are situated,
this small piece of mineralised earth
that has been worn smooth by erosion,
for I am the person formerly employed
to amuse a monarch or noble
usually by telling jokes,
singing comical songs,
or performing tricks

and they use the particular term
'Lubbert Das'
to address or refer to me.

O person who in some games has reached
a high level of achievement,
especially in chess or bridge,
without delay please nick out the seed,
the pit, the pip or kernel
that is lodged in my cranio-skeletal caput,
in order to correct what might otherwise be
a misleading impression that I am
a comic performer usually in a circus
who does not speak and wears
an outlandish costume and heavy makeup
and who goes by the uncomplimentary
or abusive word or phrase
used to describe somebody such as this:
'Lubbert Das'.

O man in a position of authority
e.g. over a business or servants,
who controls or influences events or other things,
would you put yourself into that state
in which somebody moves
or does something with great speed
because that dimension which enables us
to measure the interval between two events
is short,
and remove from the section of my body
that is forward of all other segments

a piece of rock that has been shaped
by geological processes,
for I am that somebody or something
who has been given the name
of an ill-mannered or ineffectual person:
Lubbert Das.

O man who is a teacher, especially in a school,
or whom we address with this title as a religious leader,
can I cause you to move increasingly quickly
and chop out of the highest, uppermost,
or foremost part of me
this small hard mass of mineral material
that has formed in one of my organs
(such as the kidney or gall bladder
but which, in this case, is inside
the controlling centre of my nervous system
that is connected to the spinal cord
and which consists of a mass of nerve tissue
regulating my bodily activities),
for I am said to be somebody
who behaves comically,
a practical joker described or thought of
in the particular way:
Lubbert Das.

O person who is highly skilled in a trade or craft
and is qualified to teach apprentices,
please move, act, or proceed with haste
and hack out the small hard mass
that is stuck in that part of me which is

the centre of human faculties of intellect,
emotion and reasoning,
for I am only somebody *considered to be*
or *made to appear* ridiculous
and the word, term, or phrase
by which I am known and distinguished
from other people or things
is Lubbert Das.

The Truth About the War

The thimble-rigger makes his golden ball
vanish with dexterity. He chants:
On my table three cups and a wand;
in my hand I hold a golden sphere—

where will it go? The ball will disappear
just like the gold in the audience's purse,
yet still they jostle forwards, gape agog,
like communicants before a twisted altar—

'*How does he do it?*' Are we all just hustles,
easy marks? In this age of snake charmers
and quacks, there are confidence artists
everywhere, passing off their tricks as truth.

Above, the vacant sky covers the credulous crowd,
the whole nation, the disinterested blue hills.

The World Egg

Notes on the Poems

CLOWN: first recorded in the mid-1500s, *clowne*—derived from *cloyne* meaning 'a rustic, boor, or peasant'—was used to describe a fool or jester. *Cloyne* itself perhaps descends from the Latin *colonus* 'husbandman, colonist, farmer'; the North Frisian *klonne* 'a clumsy person', or the Norse *klunni* 'a clumsy, boorish person'.

CLOWN IN SPACE

In September 2009, Canadian clown, Guy Laliberté, founder of the *Cirque du Soleil*, was launched into space from the Kazakhstan steppes, on board a Soyuz TMA-16 capsule attached to a Russian space rocket bound for the International Space Station.

CLOWN IN HEAVEN

The poem is an OuLiPo 'chimera'—the head, body, and tail of different beasts—bringing together spiritual texts on the nature of Heaven with historical and literary details on fools and jesters.

CLOWNS EXIT RUNNING

The name of a set clowning routine. In his essay, 'The Comic Mode', Joseph Meeker argues that Comedy is itself a strategy of ecological survival. In the poem, the rising waters and altered weather patterns point up the blindness of ecological folly.

EGG REGISTER

The Egg Gallery and Egg Register actually exist as a means of copyrighting clown costumes. See 'The World Egg' below.

THE LORD OF MISRULE

The tradition of appointing a Lord of Misrule extends back to Roman Saturnalia. The Feast of Fools (which took place across St. Stephen's Feast 26 Dec, St. John's Feast 27 Dec and Holy Innocents 28 Dec) was a burlesqued mass with braying, obscene jests, dances, indecent songs, and the ass as a central figure. Records from the 3rd century suggest that the merry reign of the king of the revels came to a sacrificial end on the altar of Saturn—hence the sacrificial twist to the poem. In the Middle Ages, the human sacrifice was replaced by the symbolic burning of an effigy.

THE FOOL ON 'THE END OF THE WORLD'

The poem uses the OuLiPo technique known as N+7, replacing the word 'world' with nouns that appear seven-nouns-on in the dictionary.

THE GARDEN OF EARTHLY DELIGHTS

The poem is an anagram, composed using only words spelled with letters from the title of this painting. Not all the possible words that could be formed are used. The poem is not an attempt to describe the painting but is, rather, an anagrammatic meditation upon its sensual imagery and erotic themes.

THE ADORATION OF THE MAGI

Perhaps the best known of Twentieth Century painting-poems is W.H. Auden's 'Musee des Beaux Arts', after another of the great Flemish master painters, Peter Breughel, and his painting *The Fall of Icarus*. Auden's poem contains the line 'In Breughel's Icarus, for instance: how everything turns away / Quite leisurely from the disaster', on which I have leant heavily in my own poem.

THE ERGOTIST

Ergot poisoning was caused by the fungus *Claviceps purpurea* which infects rye and other cereals. Known as Saint Anthony's Fire, or *ignis sacer* ('holy fire'), it was responsible for numerous epidemics in the Middle Ages and, with its intense hallucinations, was a suggested explanation of bewitchment. Treated in the Antonite hospitals, the monks were also reputed to be adept healers of venereal disease—a confusion furthered in the sexual connotations of fire. Athanasius wrote a Life of Saint Anthony, and the poem explores Bosch's tryptich *The Temptation of Saint Anthony* (Museu Nacional de Arte Antiga, Lisbon).

JEROEN VAN AKEN

Very little is known of Bosch's life, other than his piety. What is known comes from brief references to him in the municipal records of Hertogenbosch, from accounts of the Brotherhood of Our Lady, and from interpretations of his art. Nothing is known about his views on his own work.

THE FOREST THAT HEARS AND THE FIELD THAT SEES

The title of the poem is taken from a drawing by Bosch, which depicts a Flemish proverb: *The field has eyes, the wood has ears. I will see, keep silent and listen.* For Bosch, nature was 'fallen creation' and therefore never benign or simply indifferent. The double-edged imagery in the poem is also based upon Bosch's painting *St John the Baptist in the Wilderness* (the Prado,Madrid).

THE DEPARTURE

The two elegiac sonnets for my father take inspiration from Bosch's paintings of penitent saints: *Saint Jerome* (Palazzo Ducale, Venice); *Saint John in Patmos* (State Museum, Berlin); *Saint Jerome in Prayer* (Museum voor Schone Kunsten, Ghent), and *The Temptation of Saint Anthony* (the Prado, Madrid). The 'plenitude of bliss' is from Meister Eckhart and to 'get away from Earth a while' from Robert Frost's poem 'Birches'.

THE HAYWAIN

After Bosch's *The Haywain* (the Prado, Madrid). Tolnay argues that the painting is predicated upon the proverb which serves as the epigram to this poem.

THE SHIP OF FOOLS

Bosch's painting of this name hangs in the Louvre, Paris, and is perhaps based upon the *Blau Schuyt*—the Blue Boat carnival Fellowship—or a seminal work of the time, the *Narrenschiff* by Sebastian Brant, 1494. When Bosch's monk and nun set off in their *Ship of Fools*, it is pertinent to read an environmental metaphor in the Nero-like responses of the fools who do not even realise that their vessel is doomed.

ECCE HOMO

The painting is housed at the *Städelsches Kunstinstitut* in Frankfurt. The first half of the poem responds directly to the painting, whilst the second half of the poem—symbolic of the crucifixion—details the range of man's inhumanity to his fellows through common methods of execution from history. The two lines in Latin are inscriptions appearing on the painting itself.

FOOLS FOR CHRIST

'Holy Fool' applies to any figure who behaves in unorthodox, perhaps even 'mad' ways, to mark their piety, including certain Christian Saints, Hindu Sadhus, Sufi Whirling Dervishes, the Eastern Orthodox *yurodivy*, and others. 'Fools for Christ' enact their piety in recognition of Christ's humiliation in front of the crowd and have an obvious relevance to Bosch's representations

[83]

of folly, and his paintings of the humiliated Christ. 'Crazy for God' is one of the slogans of the Unification Church—the Moonies.

THE SEVEN DEADLY ENGLYNION

Englynion are traditional Welsh and Cornish poems, usually syllabic in nature with rigid patterns of rhyme. The seven englynion here are written after Bosch's *The Seven Deadly Sins and the Four Last Things* (The Prado, Madrid), which takes the form of a tabletop *tondo*—a circular *Imago mundi*—in which the seven sinful acts take centre stage, watched by the eye of god. The epigram *Cave, Cave, Deus videt* (Beware, Beware, God sees thee) is accordingly painted around the *tondo*. The picnic, wine, Pan flute and erotic out-of-doors encounter in poem III echo Bosch's *plein air* depictions of *Lust*. The *springe* in poem IV is a small hunting snare.

CHIMERAS

See 'Clown in Heaven'. The Chimera was a fire-breathing monster from Greek myth, with the head of a lion, body of a goat, and tail of a serpent. The name refers to any fabulous beast made up of parts taken from various animals. Bosch's paintings abound with hybrid bodies: half-human, half-machine. Accordingly, the poem is a chimera of two texts: a description of the war machines invented by Leonardo da Vinci in the time of Bosch; and a present-day guide to body types.

HIERONYMUS BOSCH

The tercets are composed of lines each of which is an anagram of the painter's name.

CURSE ON A WEDDING

The images in this black-humoured love sonnet are based upon Bosch's painting, *The Wedding Feast at Cana* (Rotterdam).

THE CURE OF FOLLY — A DEFINITIONAL POEM

The poem takes the nouns from the rhyme which appears on Bosch's painting *The Cure of Folly*—

> *Meester snijt die keye ras.*
> *Myne name is Lubbert Das.*
> Master, hurry, remove the stone!
> My name is [the fool] Lubbert Das.

—and replaces them with their dictionary definitions; a technique borrowed from the OuLiPo.

After Bosch's painting *The Conjuror* (Municipal Museum of Saint-Germain-en-Laye, Paris).

THE WORLD EGG

The poem represents the world egg (out of which the universe was hatched) referred to in ancient texts from the Sanskrit, Chinese, Egyptian and Finnish, as well as the Orphic Egg of creation in ancient Greek mythology. In the folklore of the Fool, the egg was the vessel from which human folly symbolically 'hatched': fools such as Pulcinella—his name meaning 'little chicken'—were born in this way. The tricorn hat of the fool, signifying that other tripartite symbol of masculinity, the penis and two testicles, symbolically turned the fool into a 'cock', a chicken, an 'egg man'. At Carnival time in the months leading up to Lent, eggs were usually in plenty. Come Carnival, when a glut in their production meant that they needed to be used up, eggs were not only cooked in pancakes but thrown in jest. For Hieronymus Bosch, the egg becomes a fragile, hollow symbol of human folly—eggs (and other thin-walled, hollow vessels) abound in his works, the egg-like Stone of Folly in Bosch's painting *The Cure of Folly* being but one example.

This visual egg poem uses only key words taken from the poems which precede it in this collection and was designed using the software of www.wordle.net. The size of the words is relative to their frequency of use in the collection.